In My Great & Unmatched Wisdom

Coloring Book & Inspirational Quotes of President Trump

Illustrations by Kevin Berggren

Published by Amazon

Copyright © Kevin Lee Berggren 2020

ISBN: 9798689207391

Please send pics of your colored pages to the author:

DJTcoloringbook@gmail.com

Make Coloring Great Again.

This is no ordinary coloring book. Donald J. Trump is no ordinary president.

I would like to personally thank President Trump for the legacy he has provided through his hard work and dedication to the greatest country on earth. For the lives he has touched through his leadership in an unparalleled time of change, turbulence yet also hope.

I have not spoken with Mr. President, or asked his permission to create this book based on his own wise utterances, but I hope that if he were to receive a copy, he would see that my intention in organizing and creating it is out of admiration and respect, for a man who is at once loved, respected, admired by many and at the same time misunderstood and unjustly reviled by others. While the collection of quotes are inspiring, provocative and at times somber, there is also of course humor – after all it is a coloring book. While Mr. Trump is intelligent, to put it mildly, it is clear from his many speeches and appearances in the media, that he also has a refined sense of humor. What good is wisdom without the ability to laugh at oneself? Or as Benjamin Franklin put it: *"If you would not be laughed at, be the first to laugh at yourself."* So, while my main wish is for President Trump to feel honored by this collection, I hope that he would also chuckle in the good natured way he often does, at the gentle humor within these pages.

My hope is that you, the reader and colorist of this book, will be inspired and heartened, by the words of a great man, to reach for the stars in your own life. To be the best version of yourself in service of your families and communities. Please be creative in your coloring and proud enough of the results to display your work for the enjoyment of yourself and others.

A note regarding the style of the drawings in this book. You'll note that I have not created the line art in the same style as most coloring books, with every shape being enclosed by a solid line that is meant to be filled with a single color. These drawings are more in the style of a comic book or graphic novel and colors are meant to be applied with more freedom, with the opportunity of blending colors and tones. My suggestion is to use colored pencils or art pens with transparent colors. Use your colored pages to inspire, or simply decorate your space, or as gifts.

Have fun, be creative, believe in freedom, be free.

Kevin Berggren

"NO DREAM is too big, NO CHALLENGE is too great.
Nothing we want for our future is BEYOND OUR REACH."

Donald J. Trump

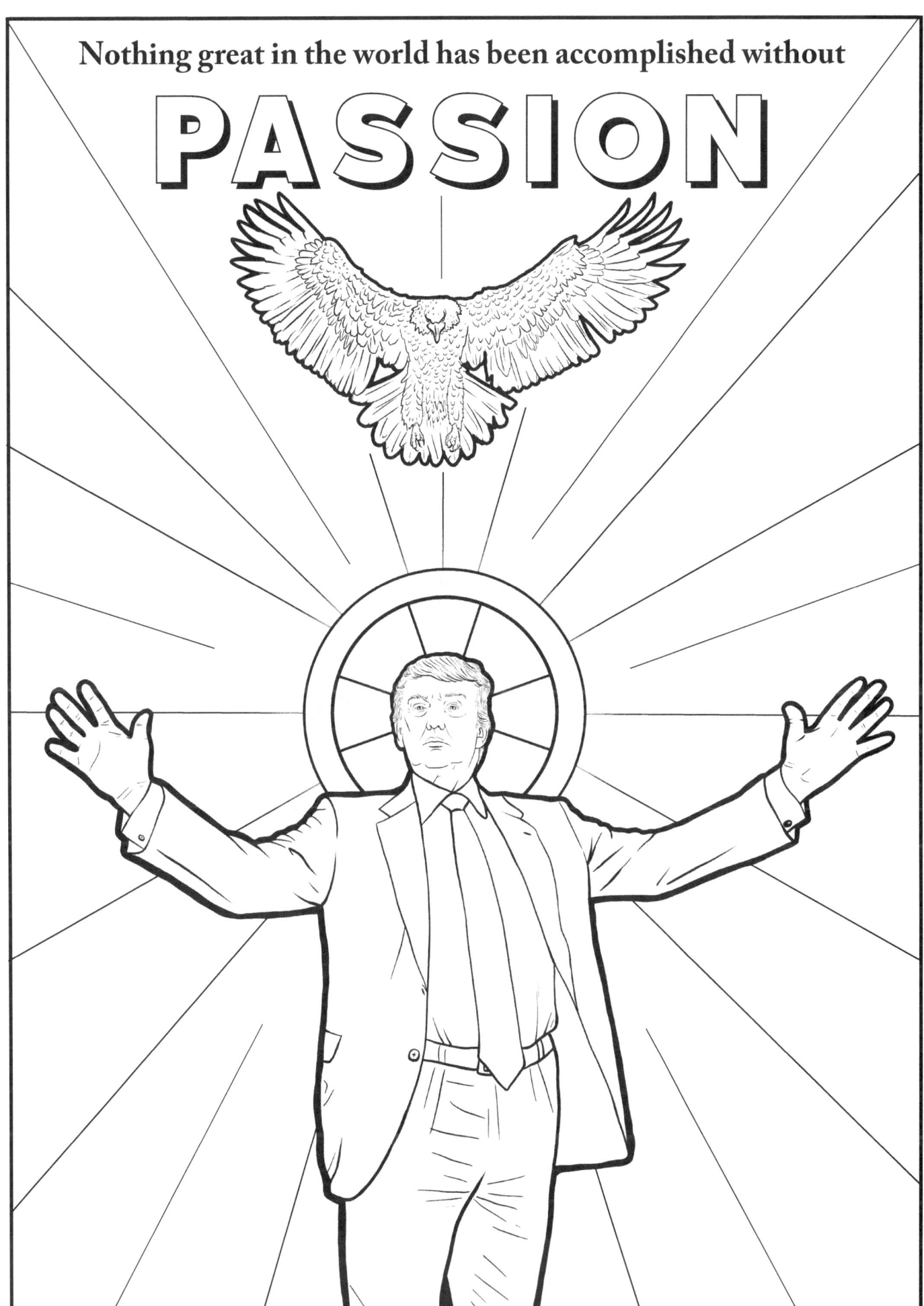

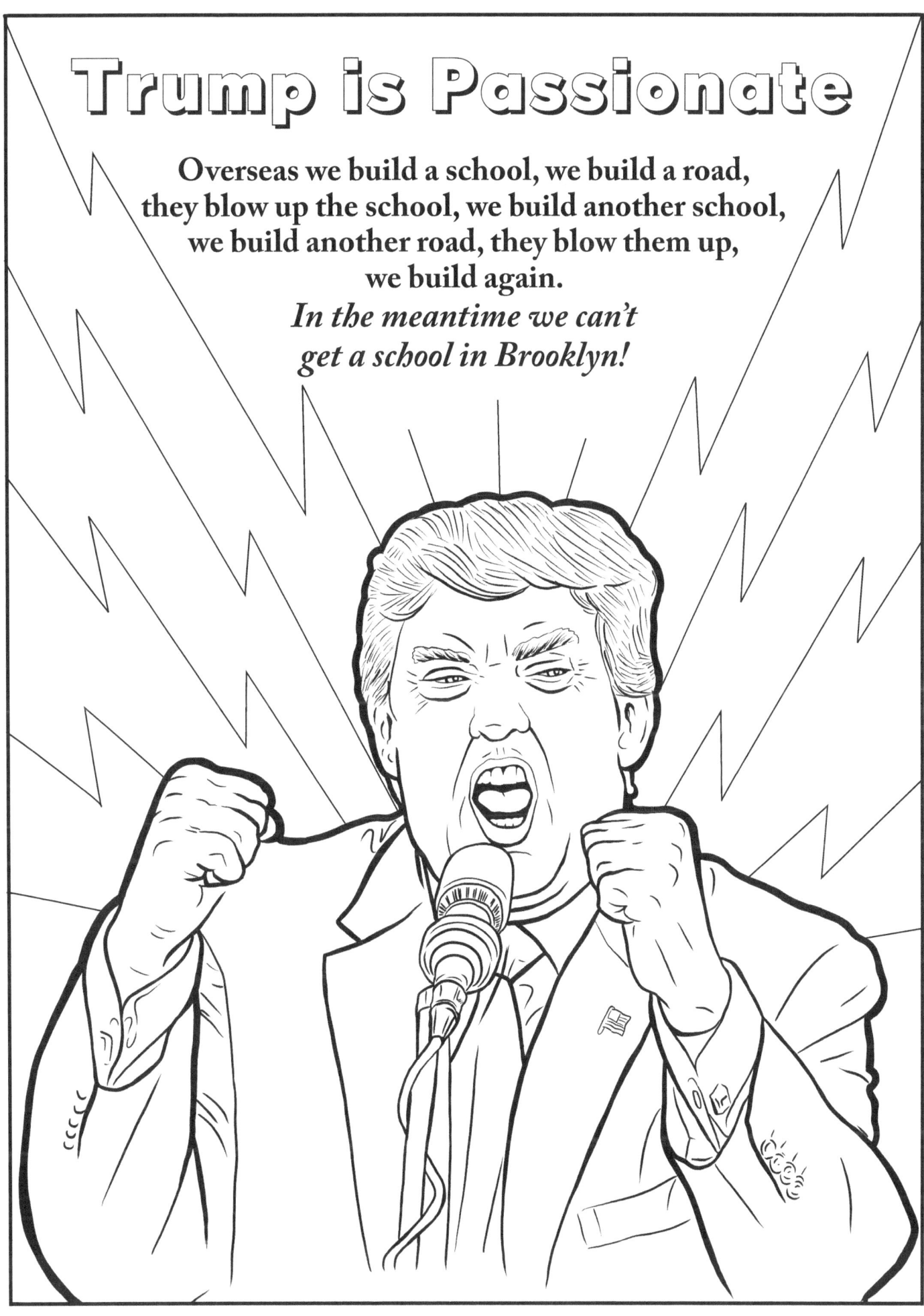

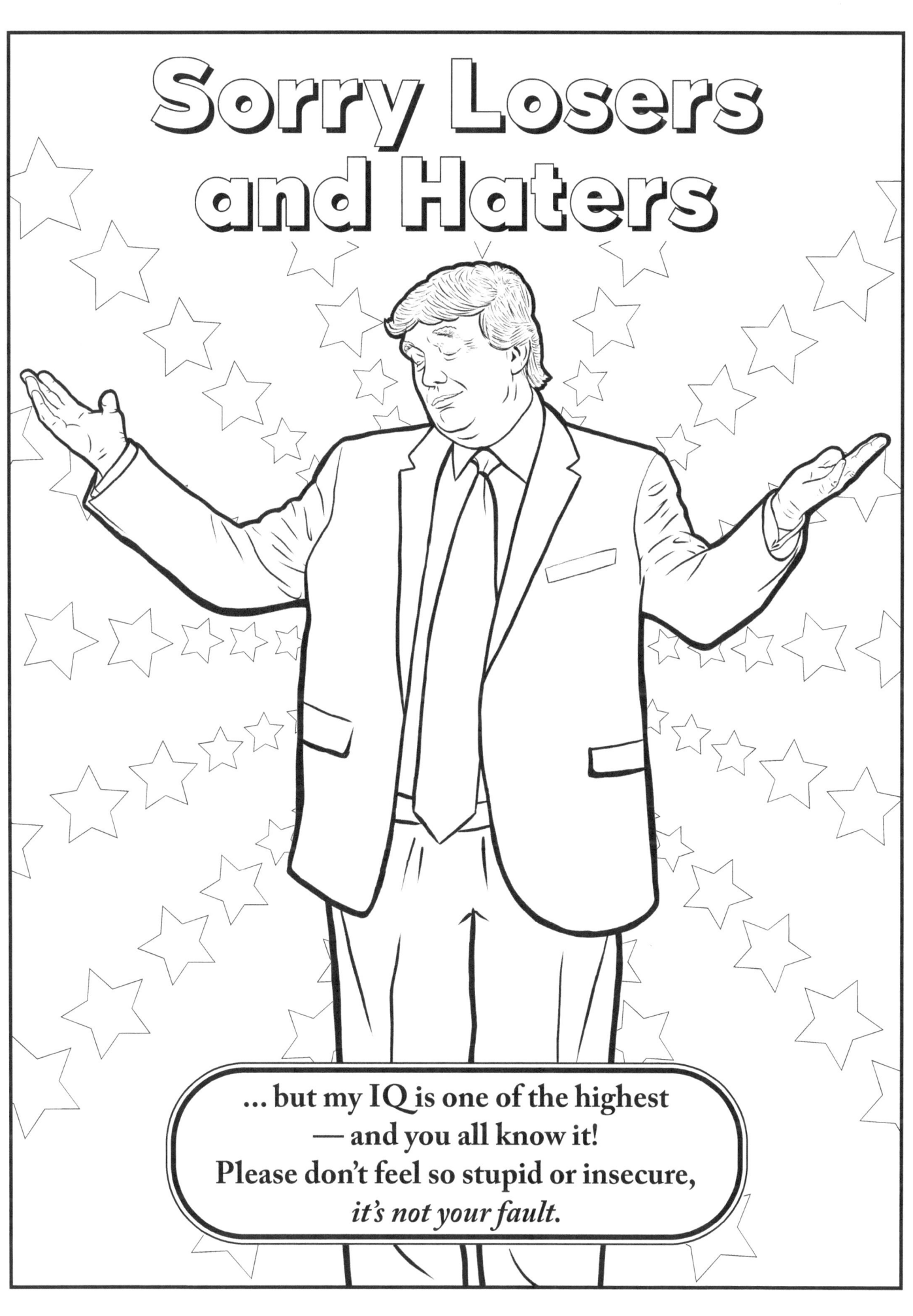

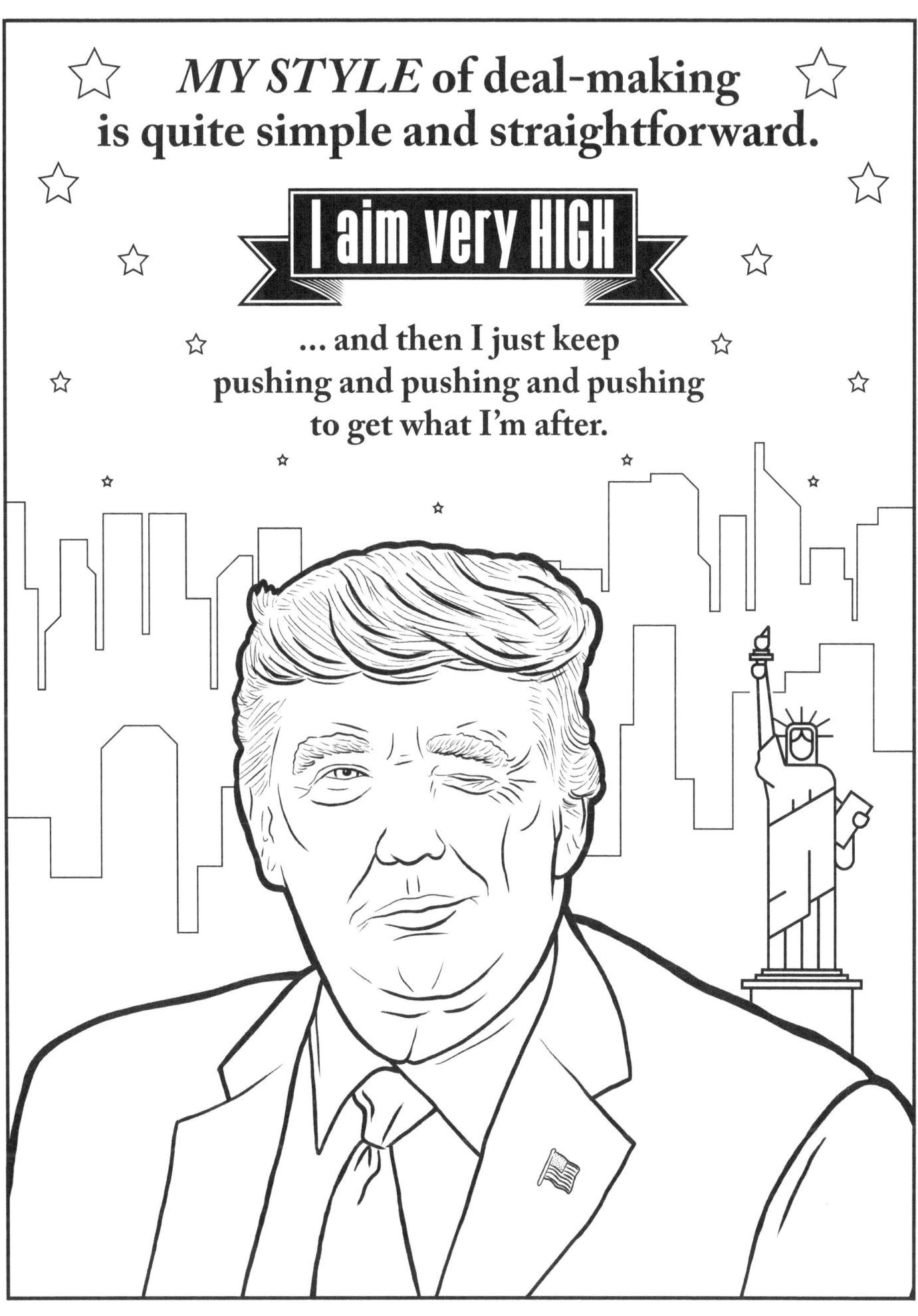

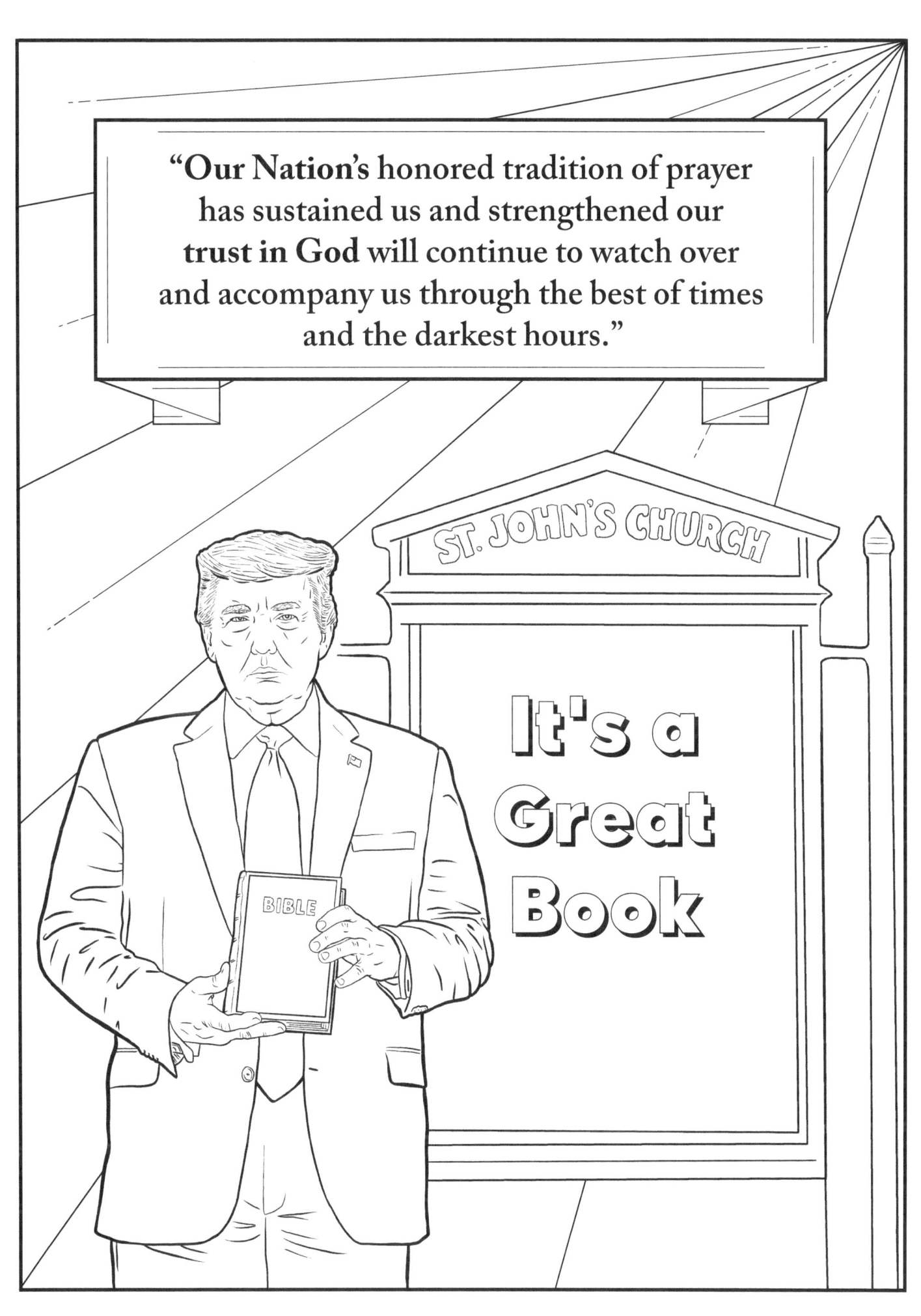

Nothing is Easy

But Who Wants Nothing?

We are responsible for our own Luck

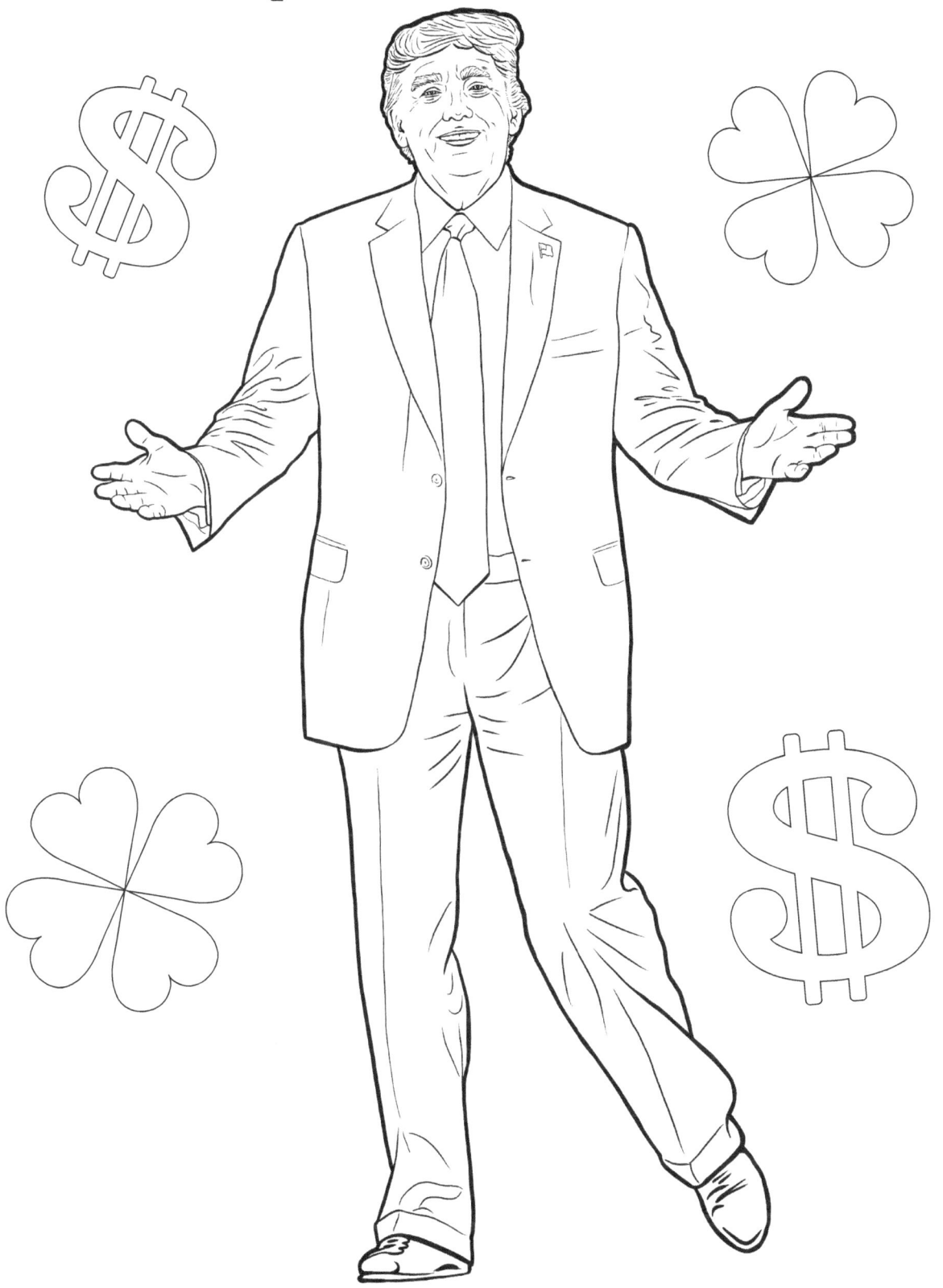

What an empowering thought! If you see responsibility as a bum deal, then you are not seeing it for what it really is – *a great opportunity.*

I like to think of the word FOCUS as:

Follow
One
Course
Until
Successful

I try to learn from the past,
but I plan for the future by *focusing*
exclusively on the present.
That's where the fun is.

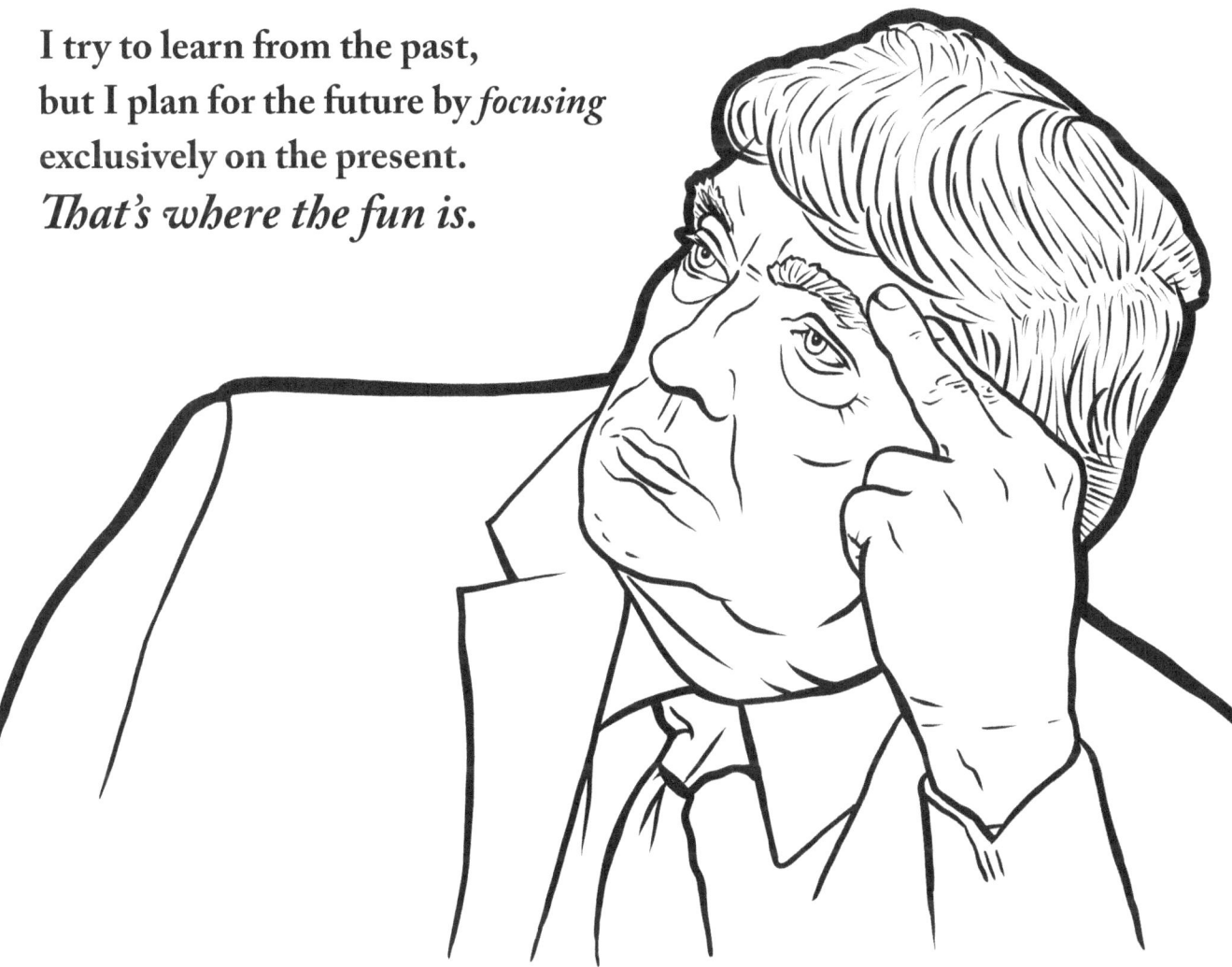

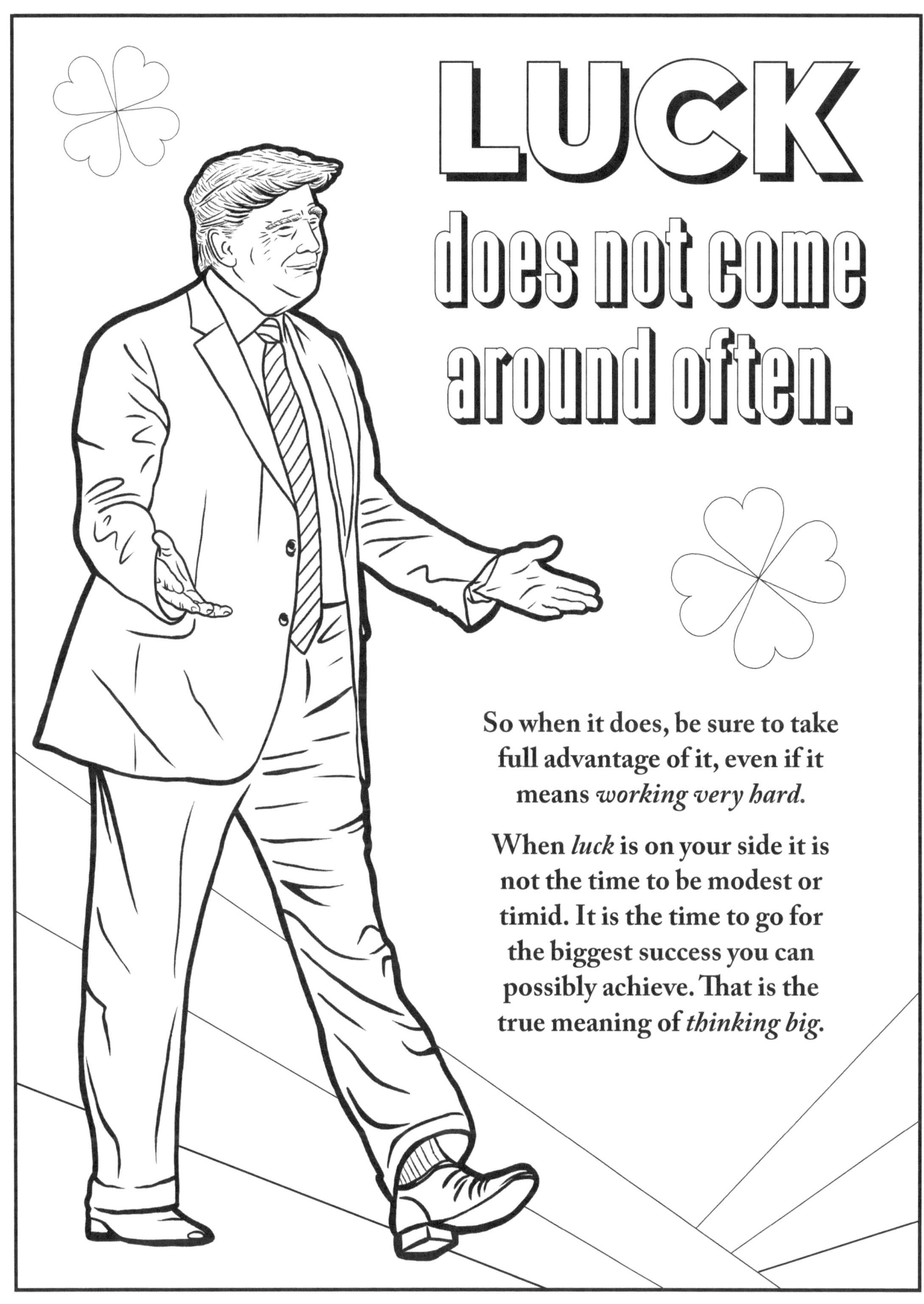

LUCK
does not come around often.

So when it does, be sure to take full advantage of it, even if it means *working very hard*.

When *luck* is on your side it is not the time to be modest or timid. It is the time to go for the biggest success you can possibly achieve. That is the true meaning of *thinking big*.

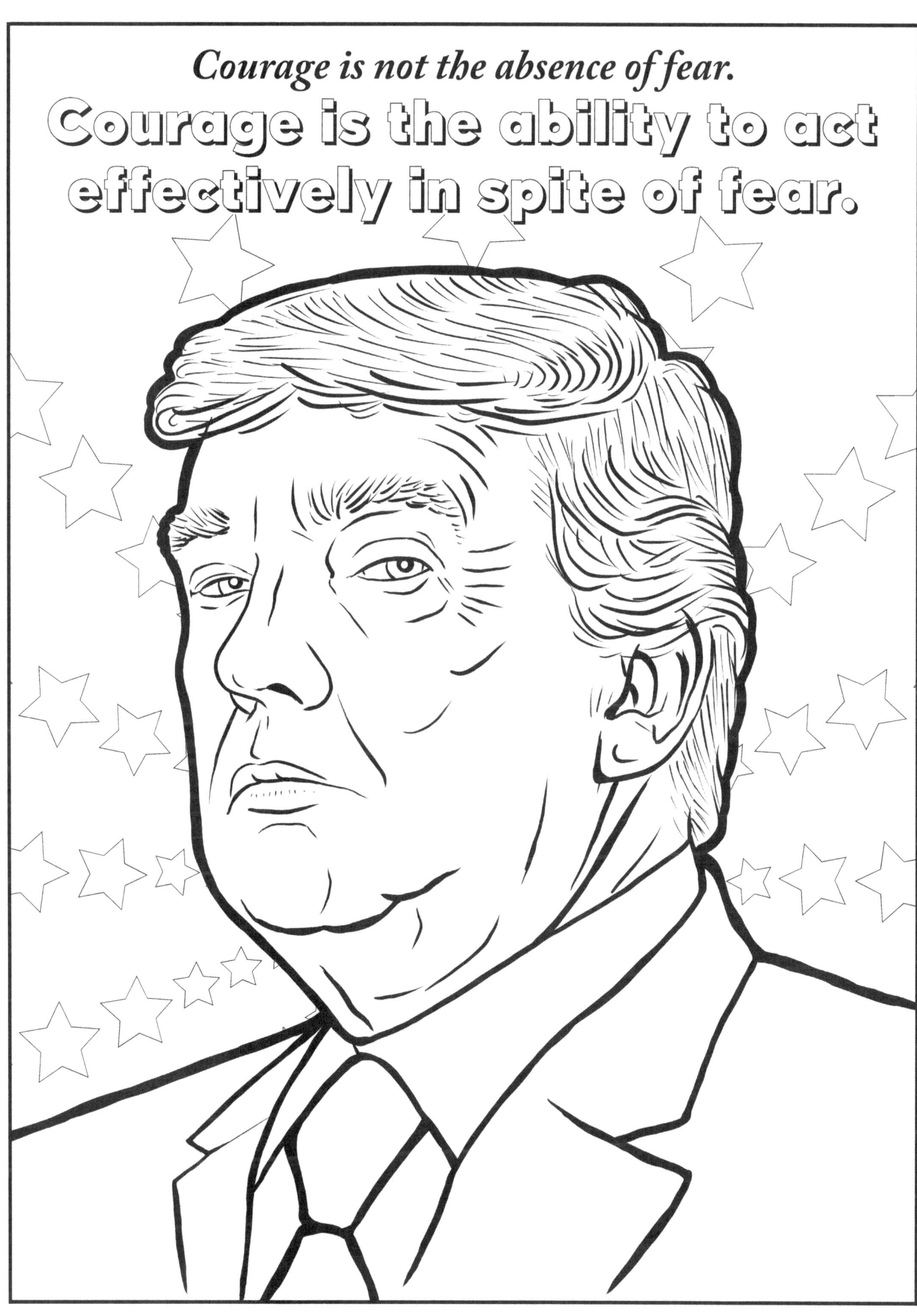

Courage is not the absence of fear.
Courage is the ability to act effectively in spite of fear.

Think BIG!

I like thinking big. I always have. To me it's very simple:

if you're going to be thinking anyway,

you might as well think big.

Most people think small, because they are afraid of success,

afraid of making decisions, afraid of winning.

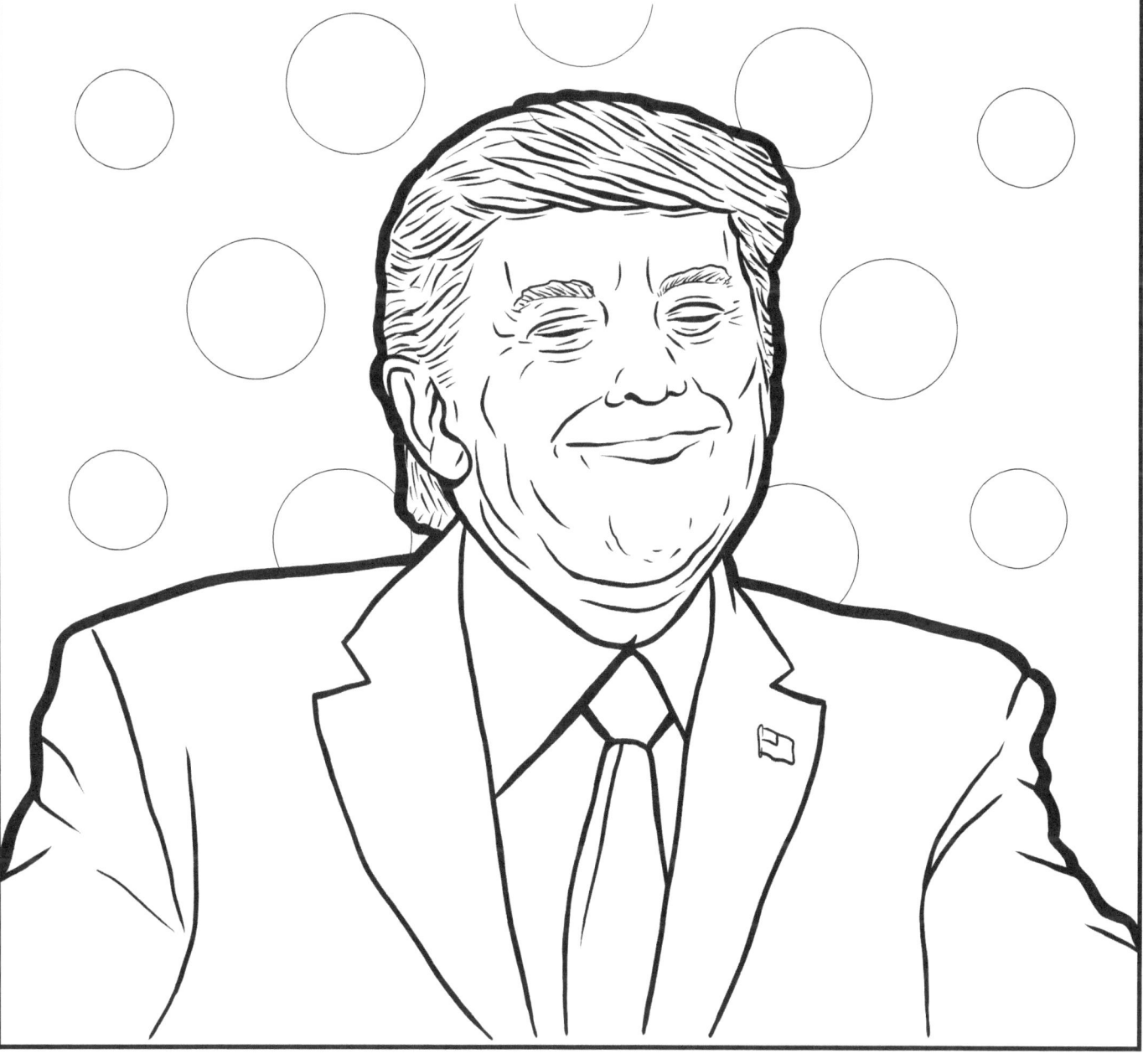

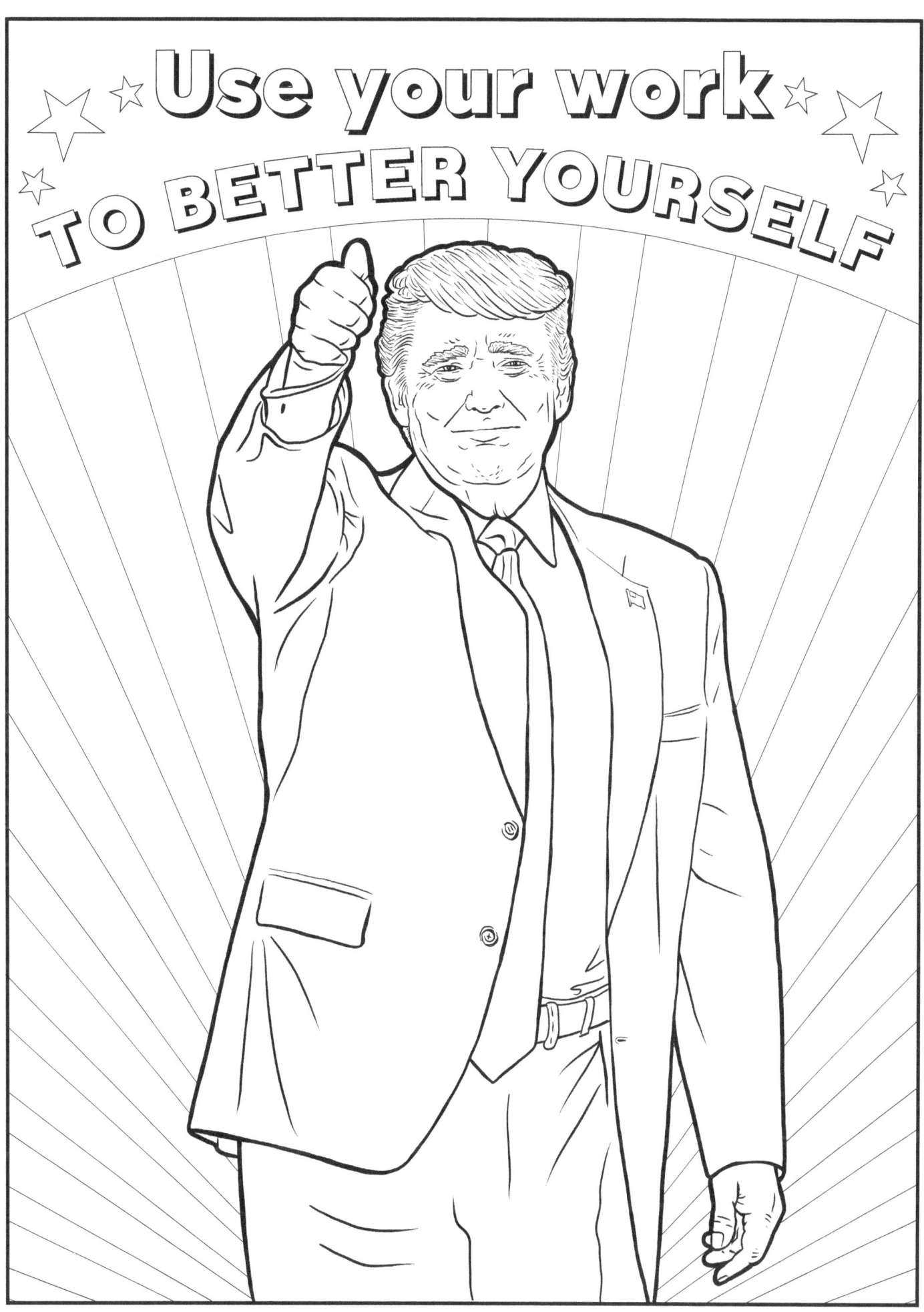

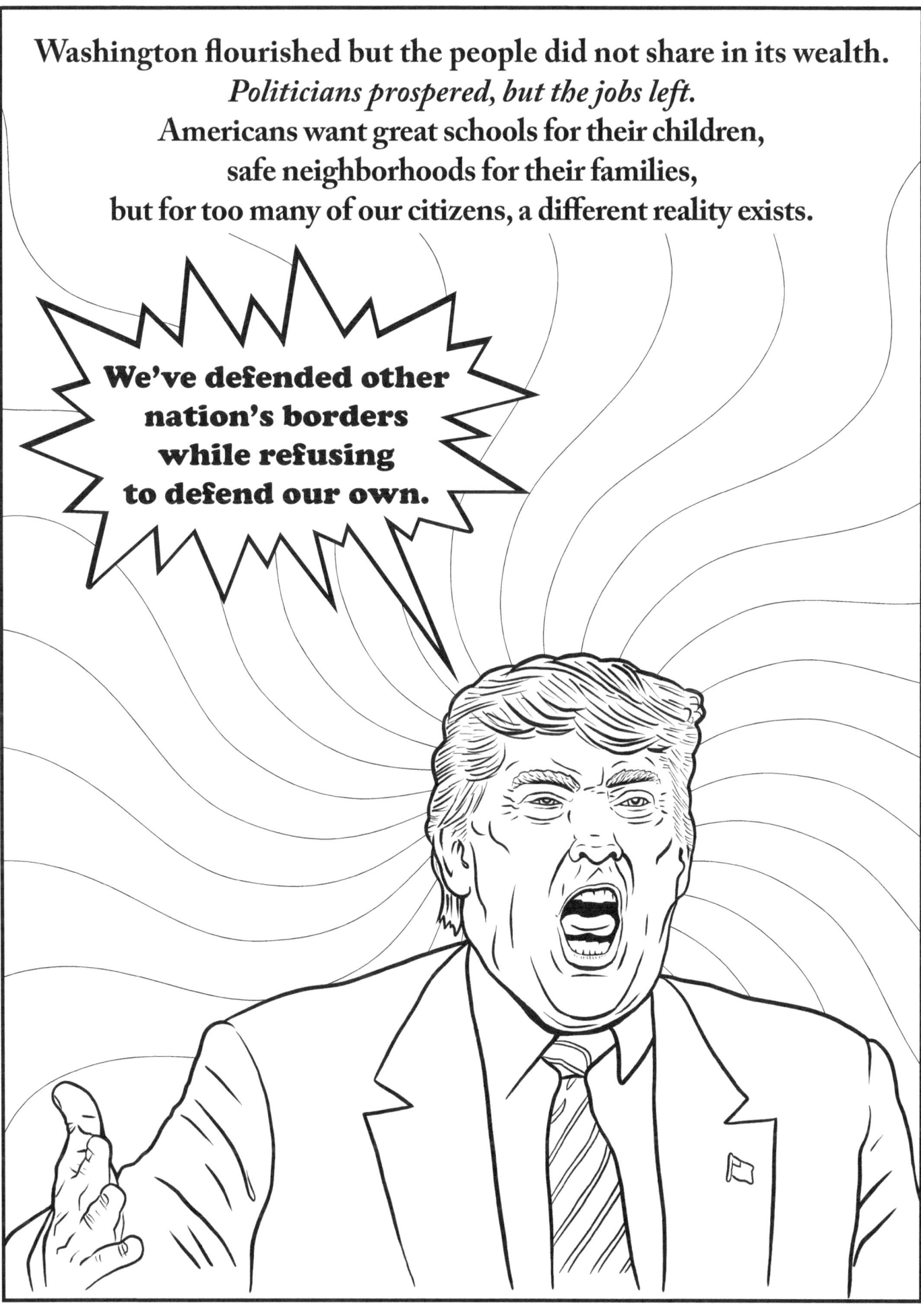

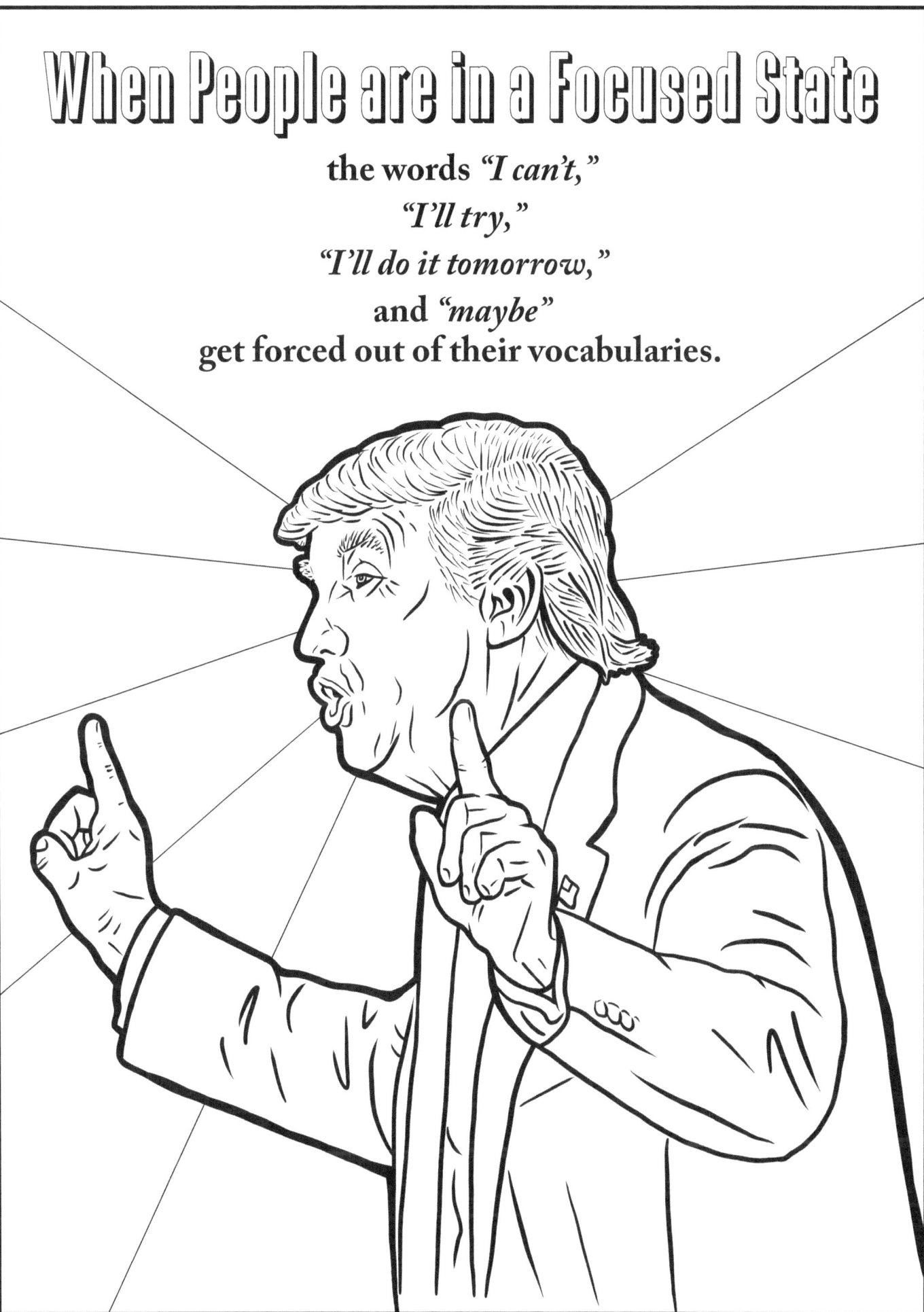

Take Blips in Stride

Instead of trying to deflect problems or obstacles and send them
off in another direction, try to embrace them.
Turn them into something positive. You can often disarm people this
way and get them on your side. Don't get too attached to your ideas.
Adjust, adapt, and take things in stride.

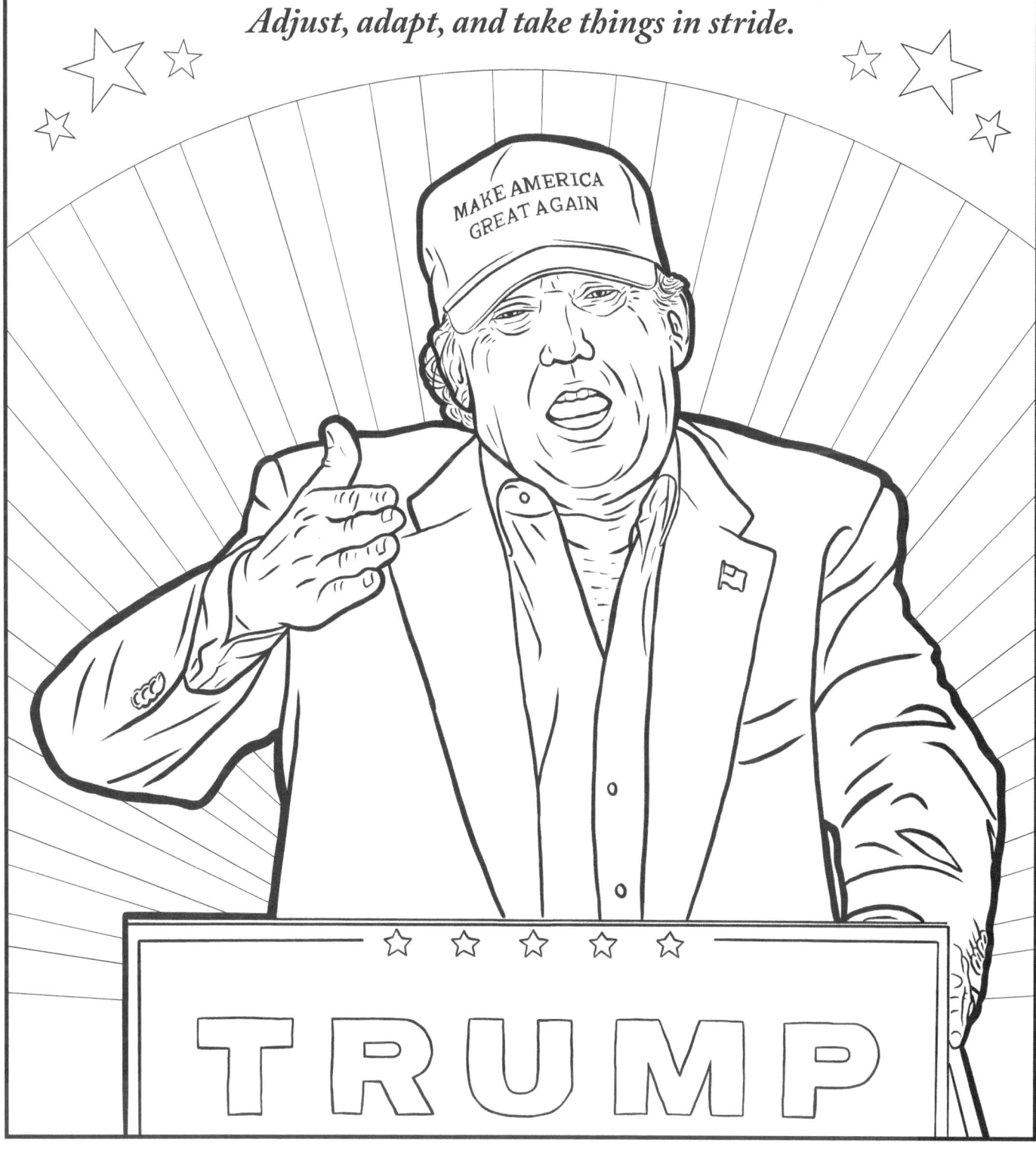

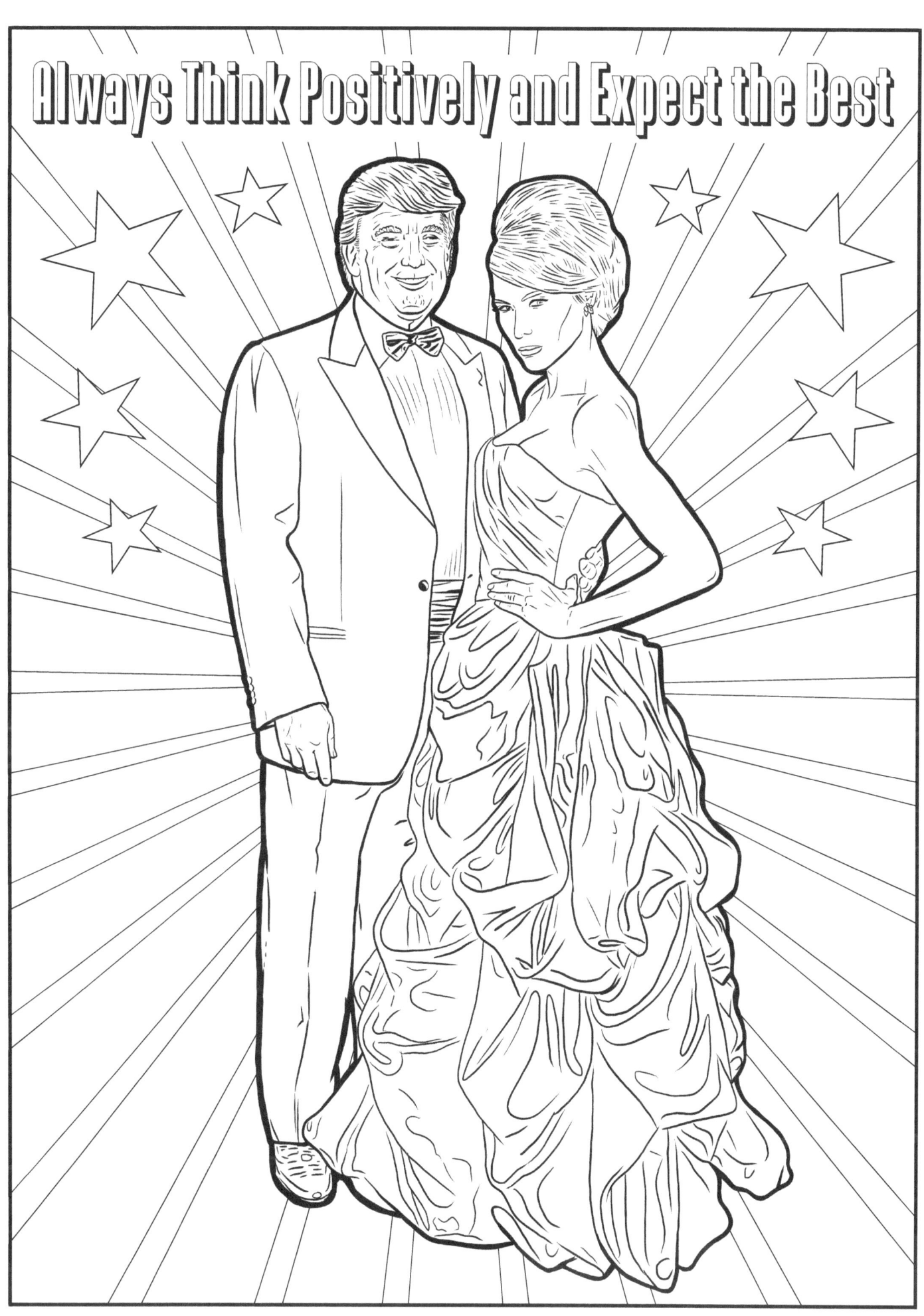

We must understand that *governments cannot create real jobs.*
Only entrepreneurs can do that.

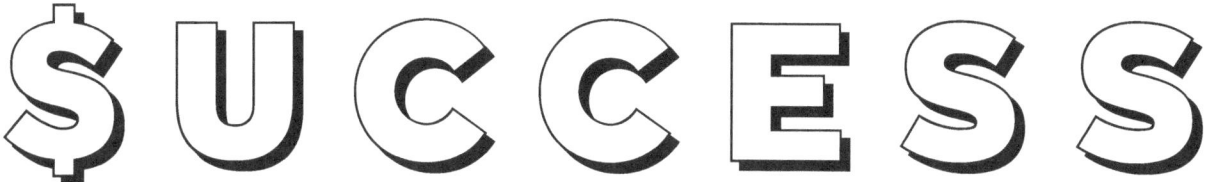

Even as entrepreneurs, we rely on people to get things done.
We may have the original idea, but moving it forward can
involve hundreds of people. Every person becomes integral
to the overall success.

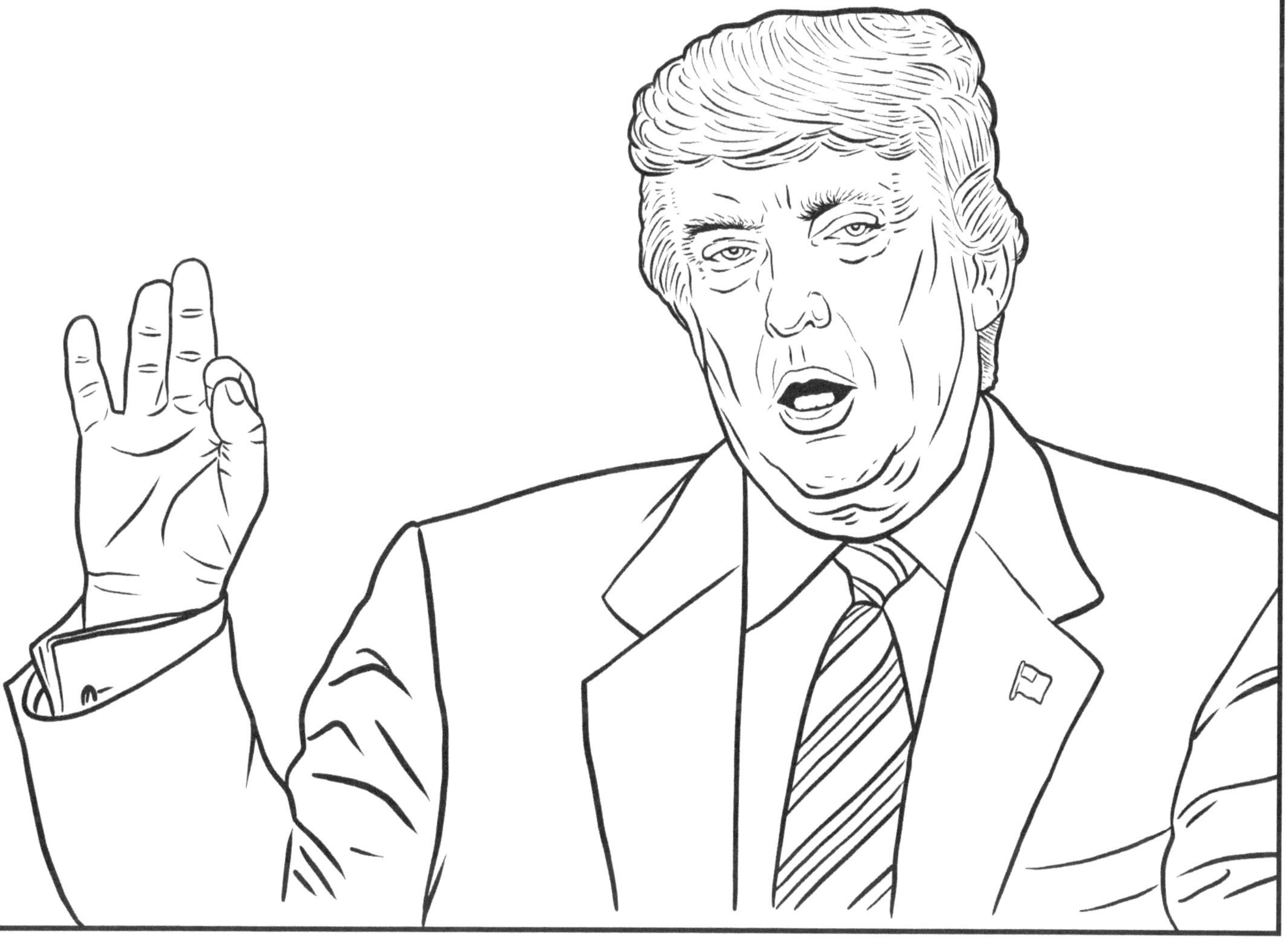

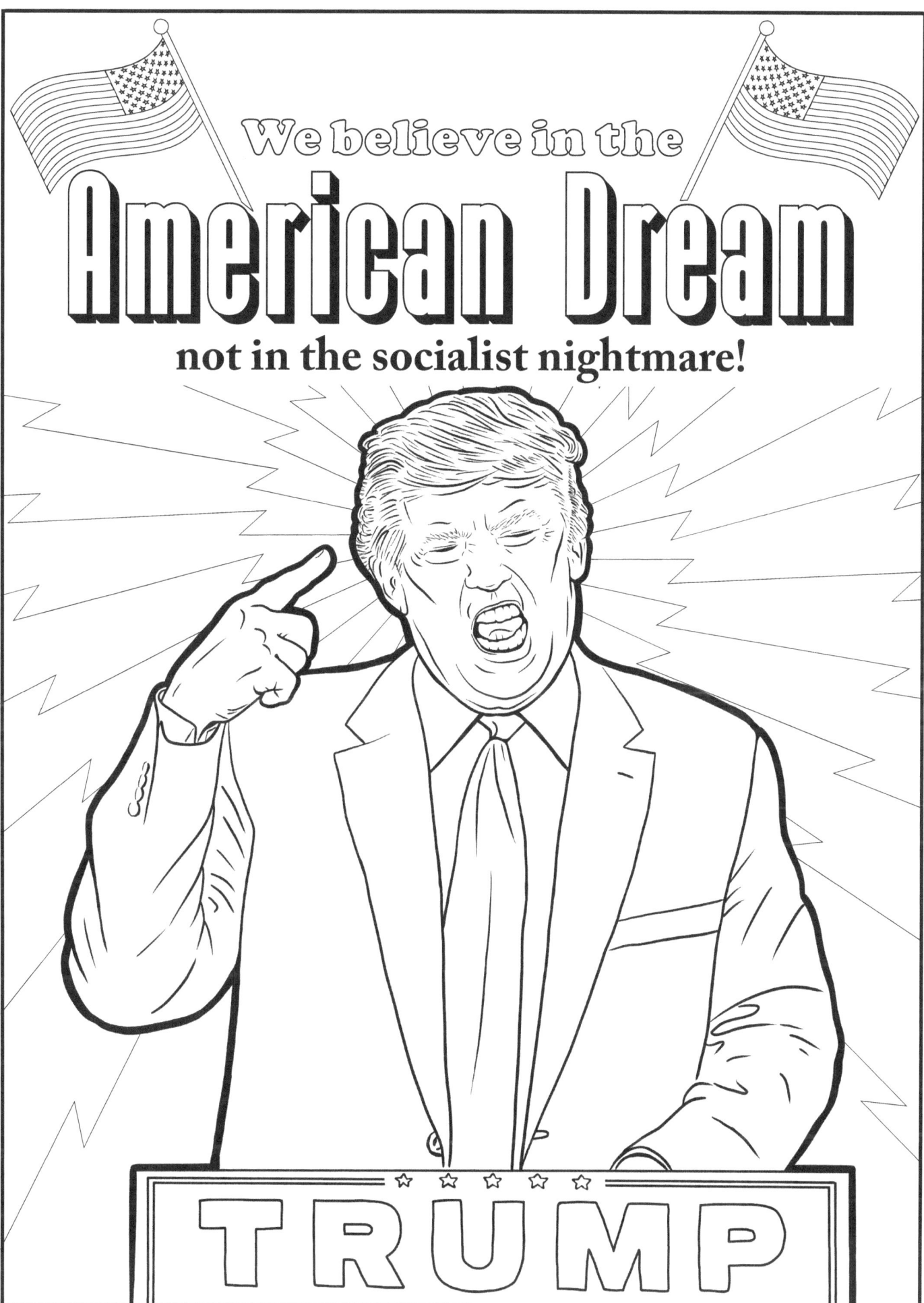

CRITICISM

is easier to take when you *realize*
that the only people who aren't criticized
are those who don't take risks.

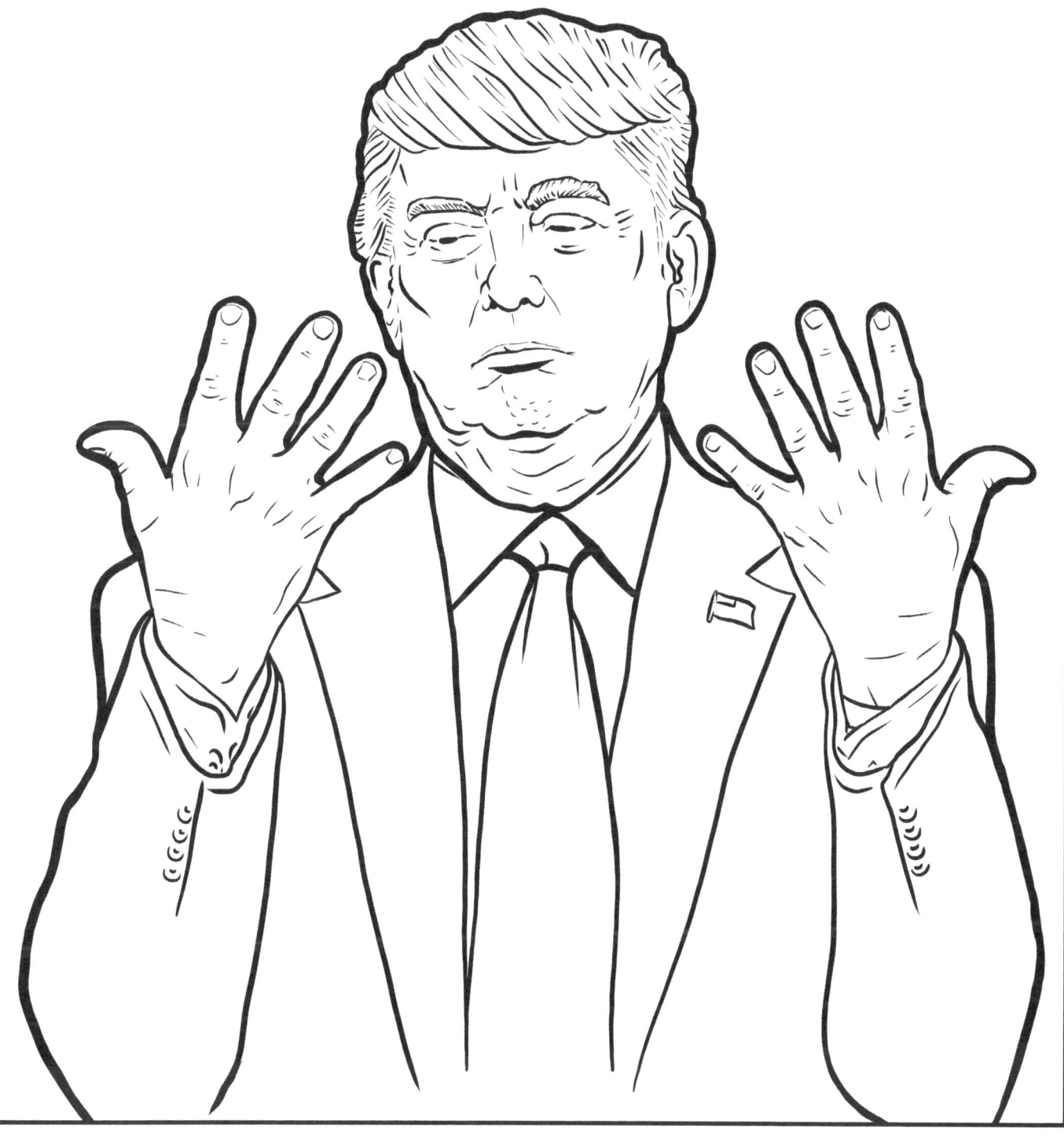

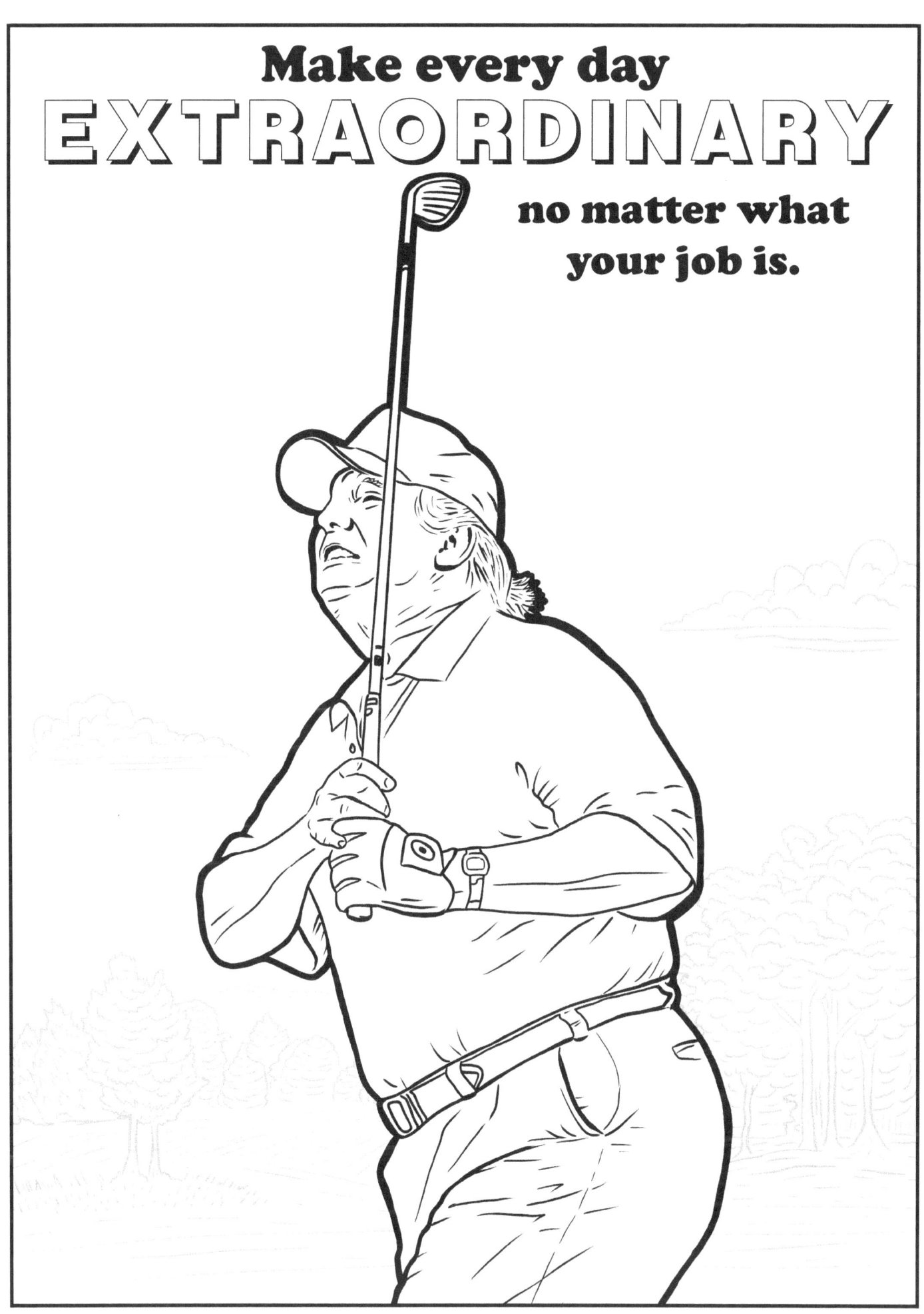

Watch, Listen, and Learn

You can't know it all yourself.
Anyone who thinks they do is destined for *mediocrity*.

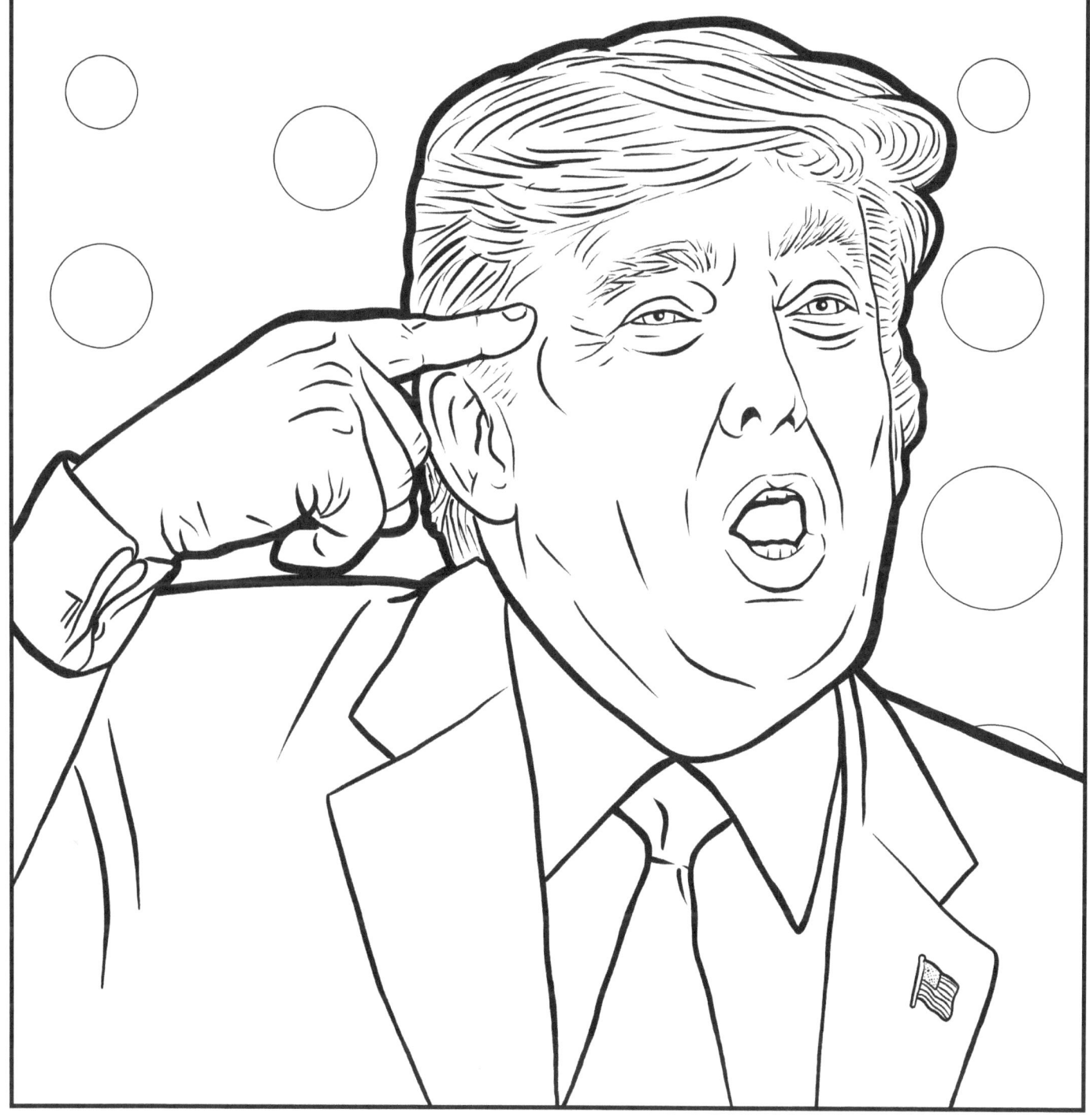

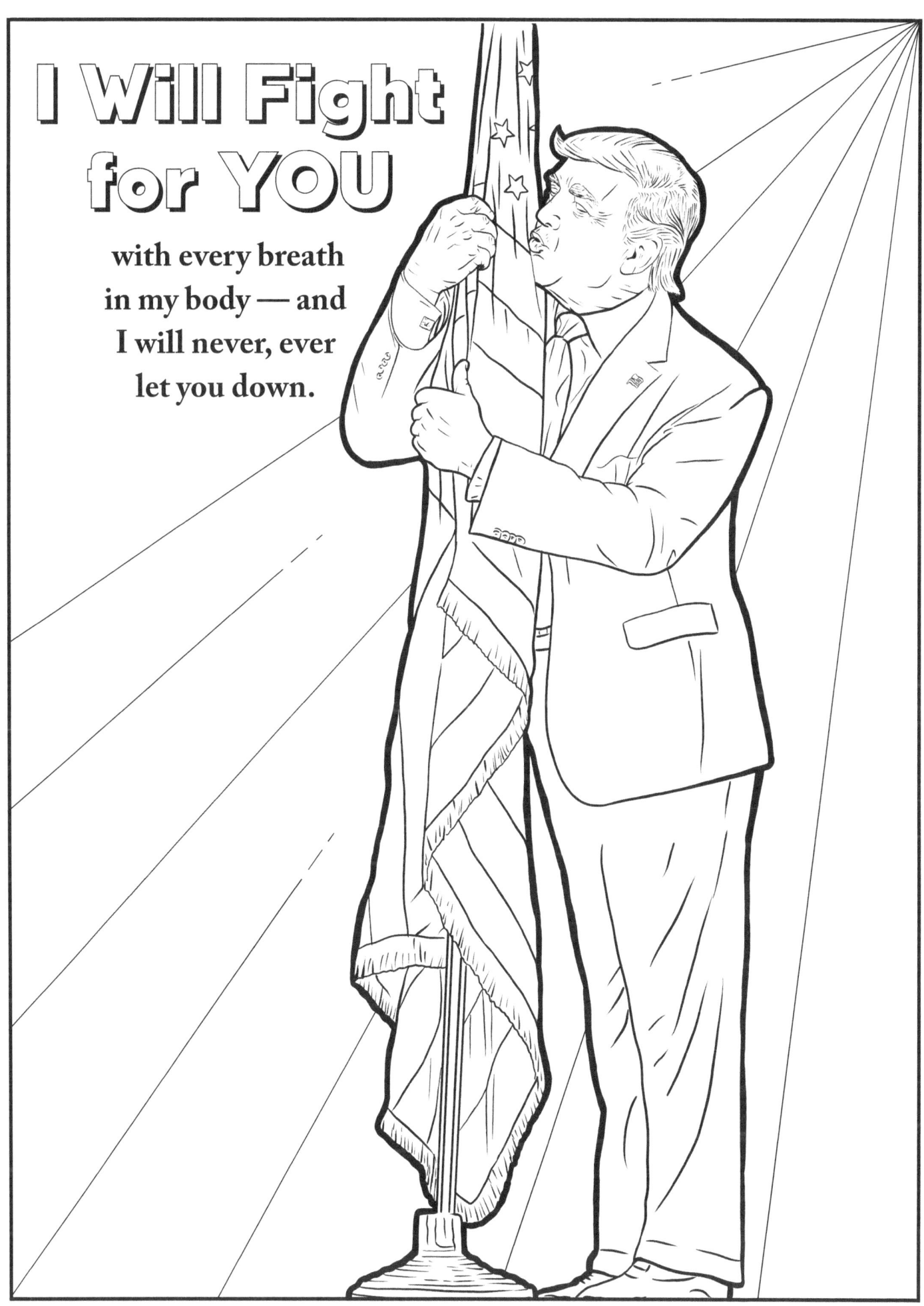

I Will Fight for YOU

with every breath in my body — and I will never, ever let you down.

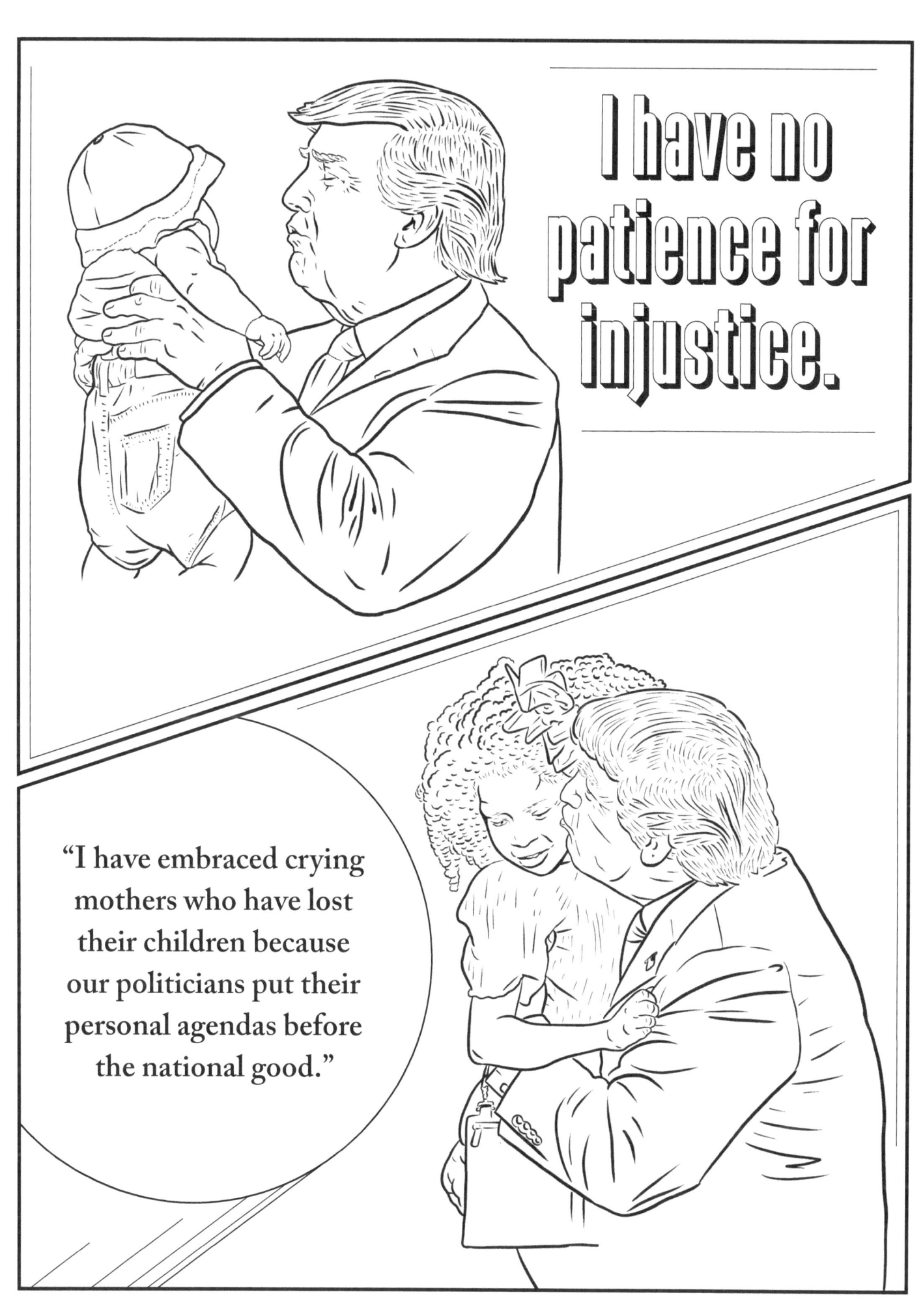

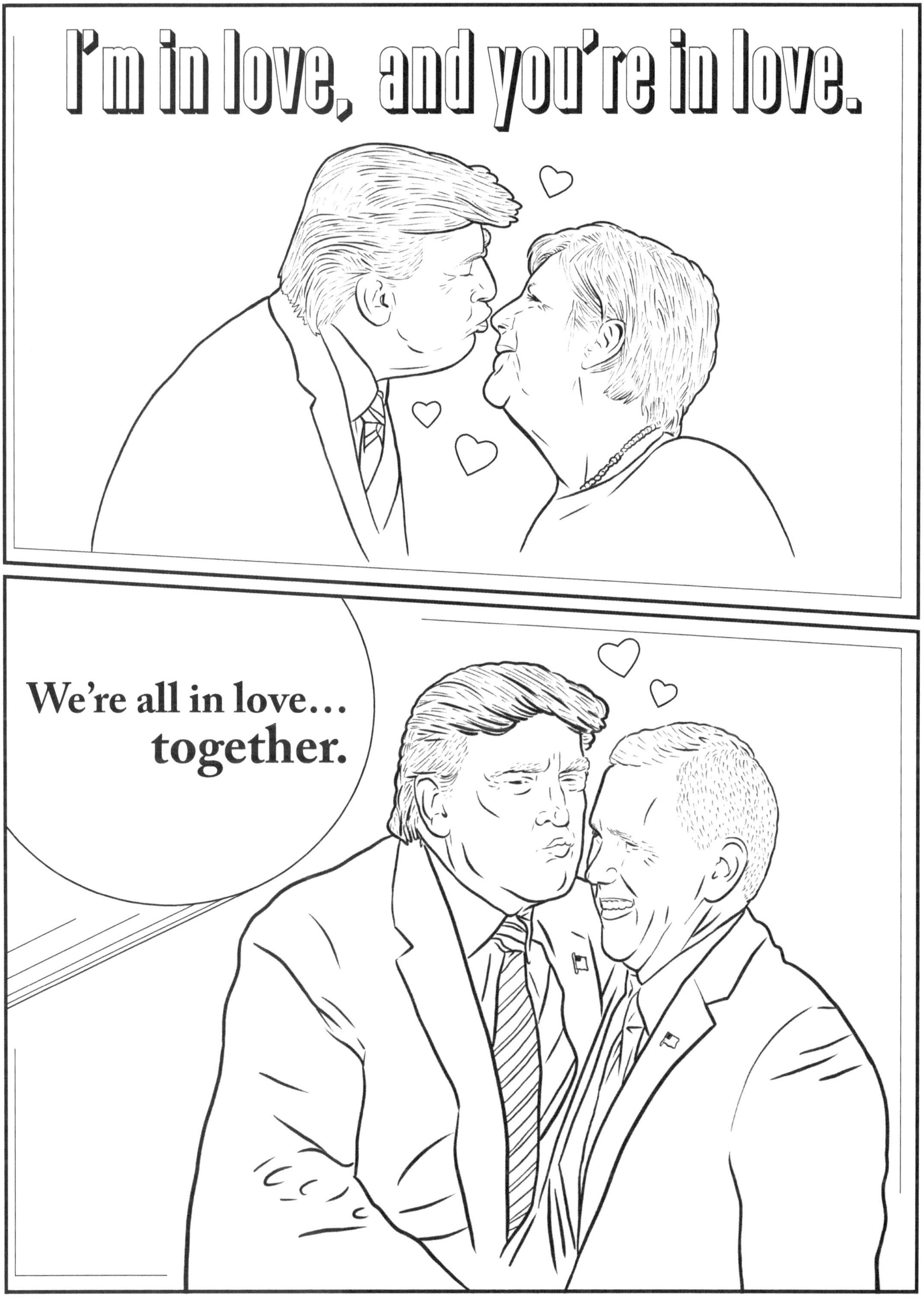
I'm in love, and you're in love.
We're all in love… together.

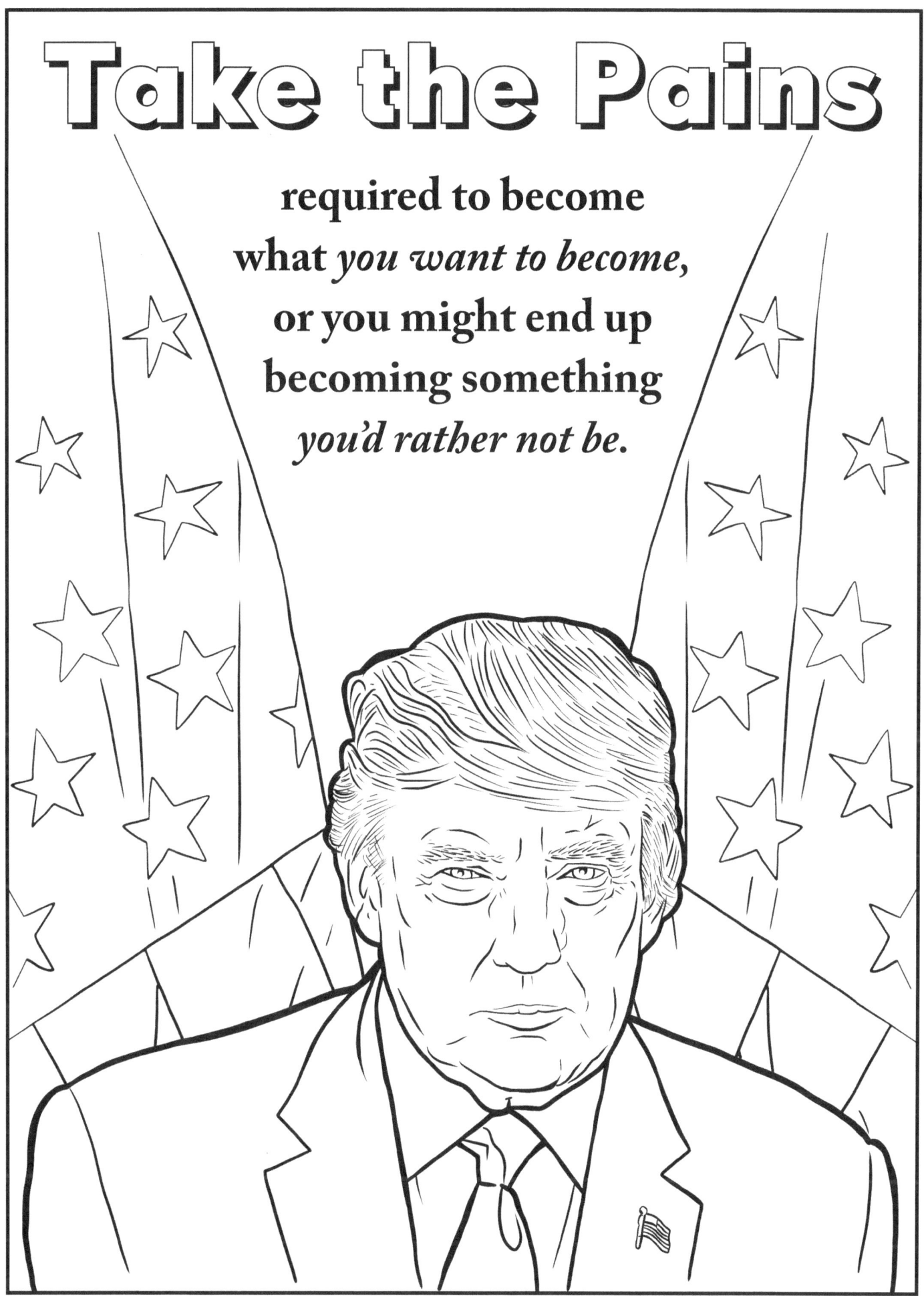

I have a great relationship with *African Americans*,
as you possibly have heard.
I just have great respect for them.

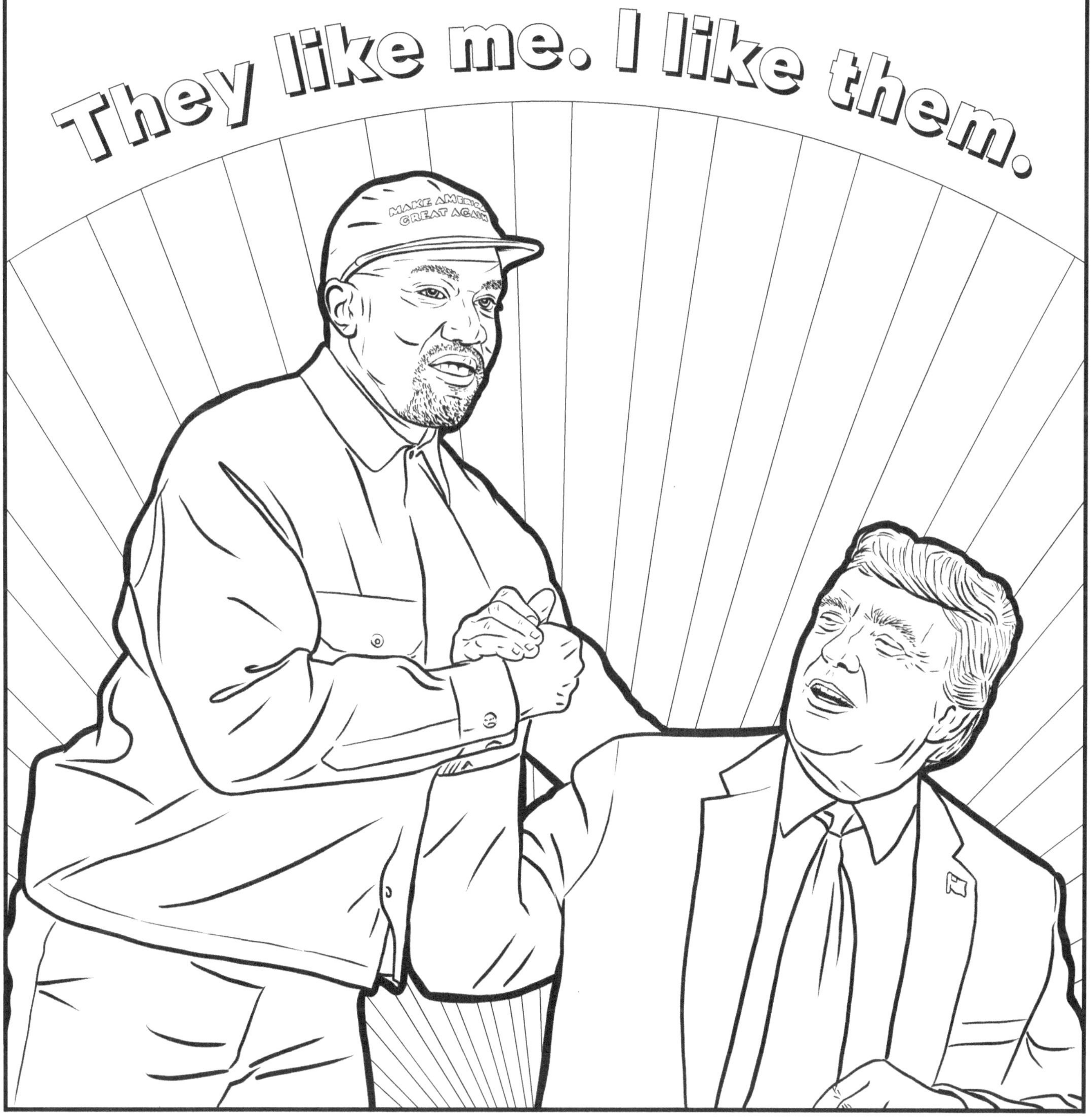

They like me. I like them.

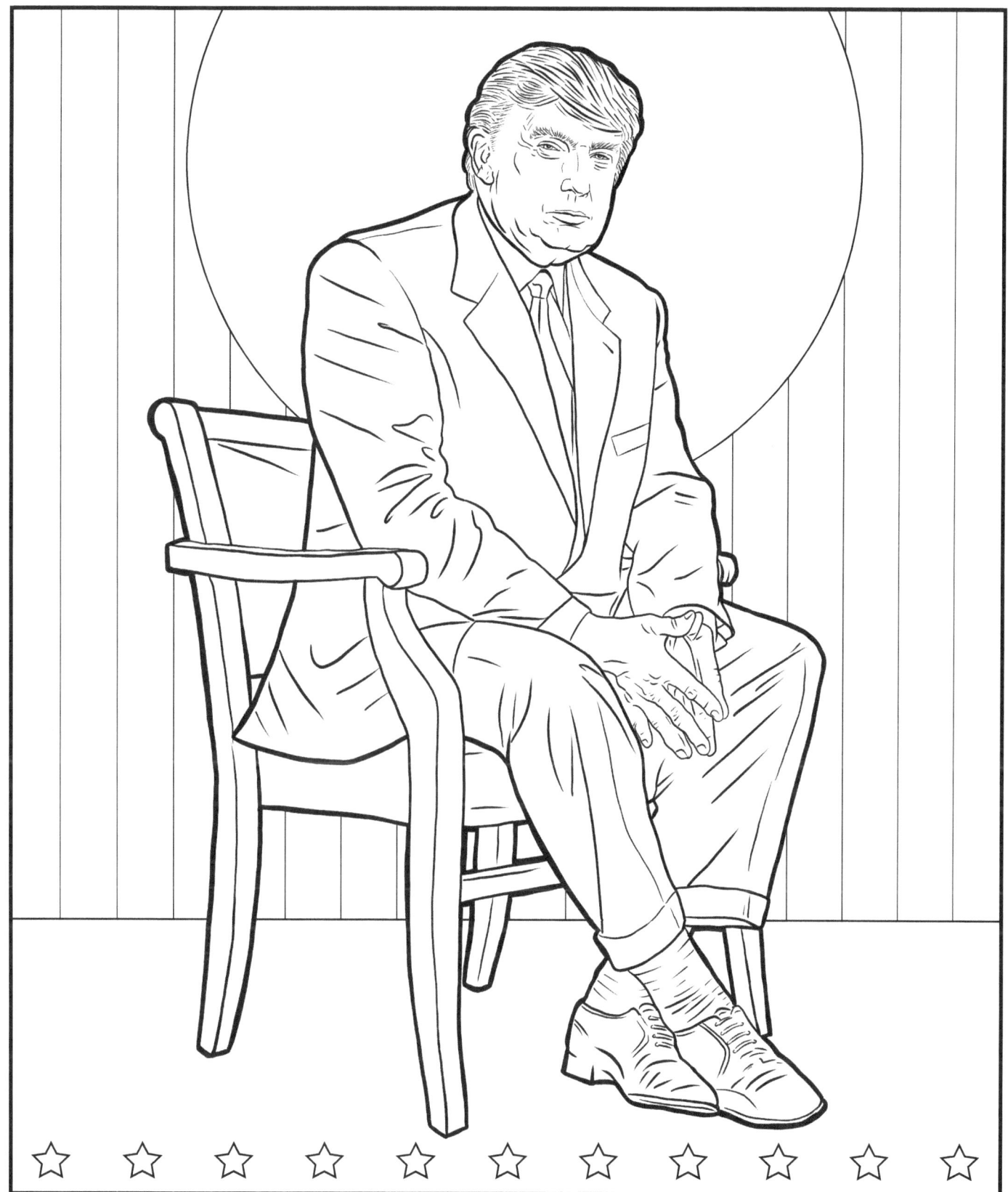

The most important thing in life is
to love what you're doing,
because that's the only way you'll ever be really good at it.

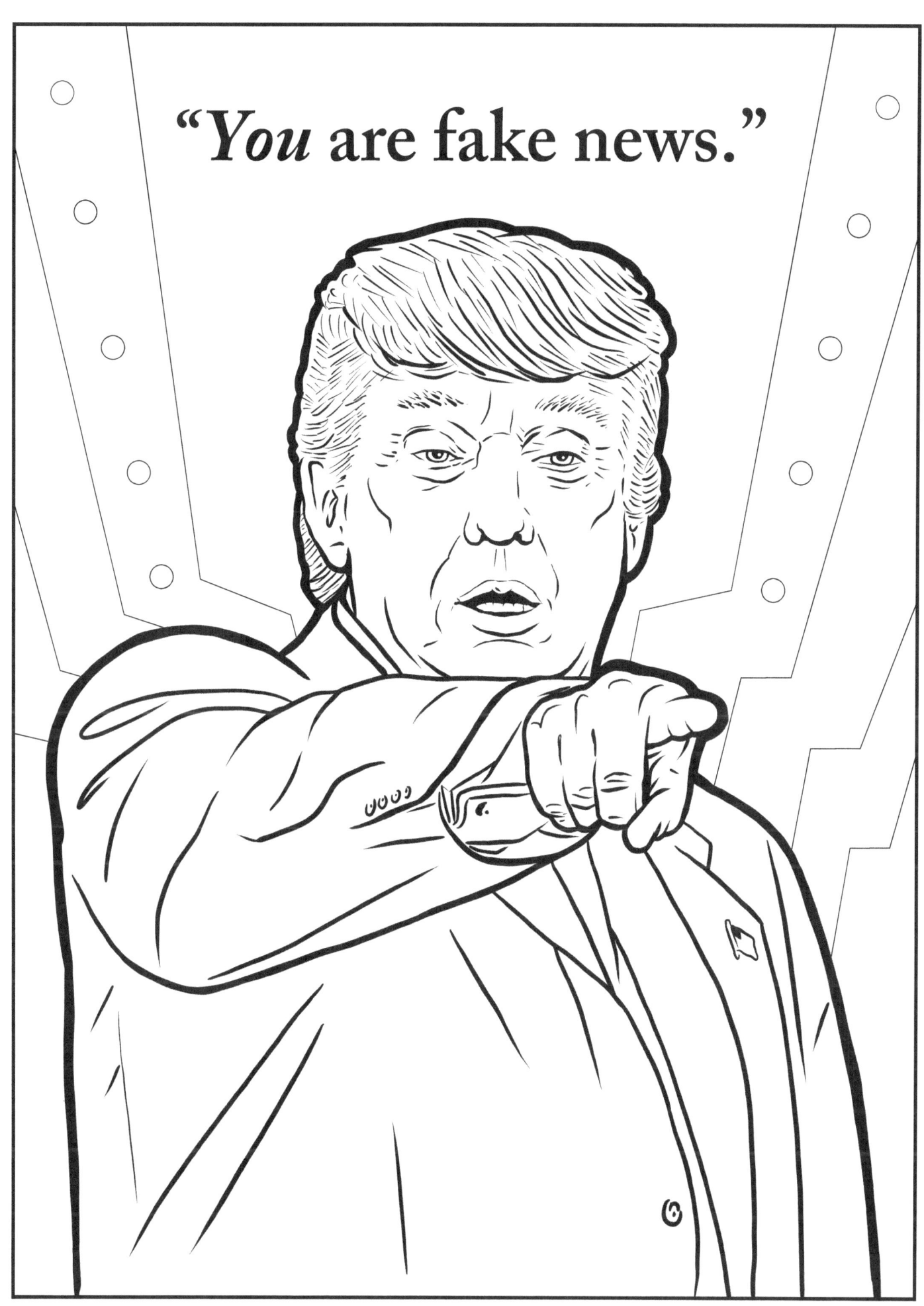

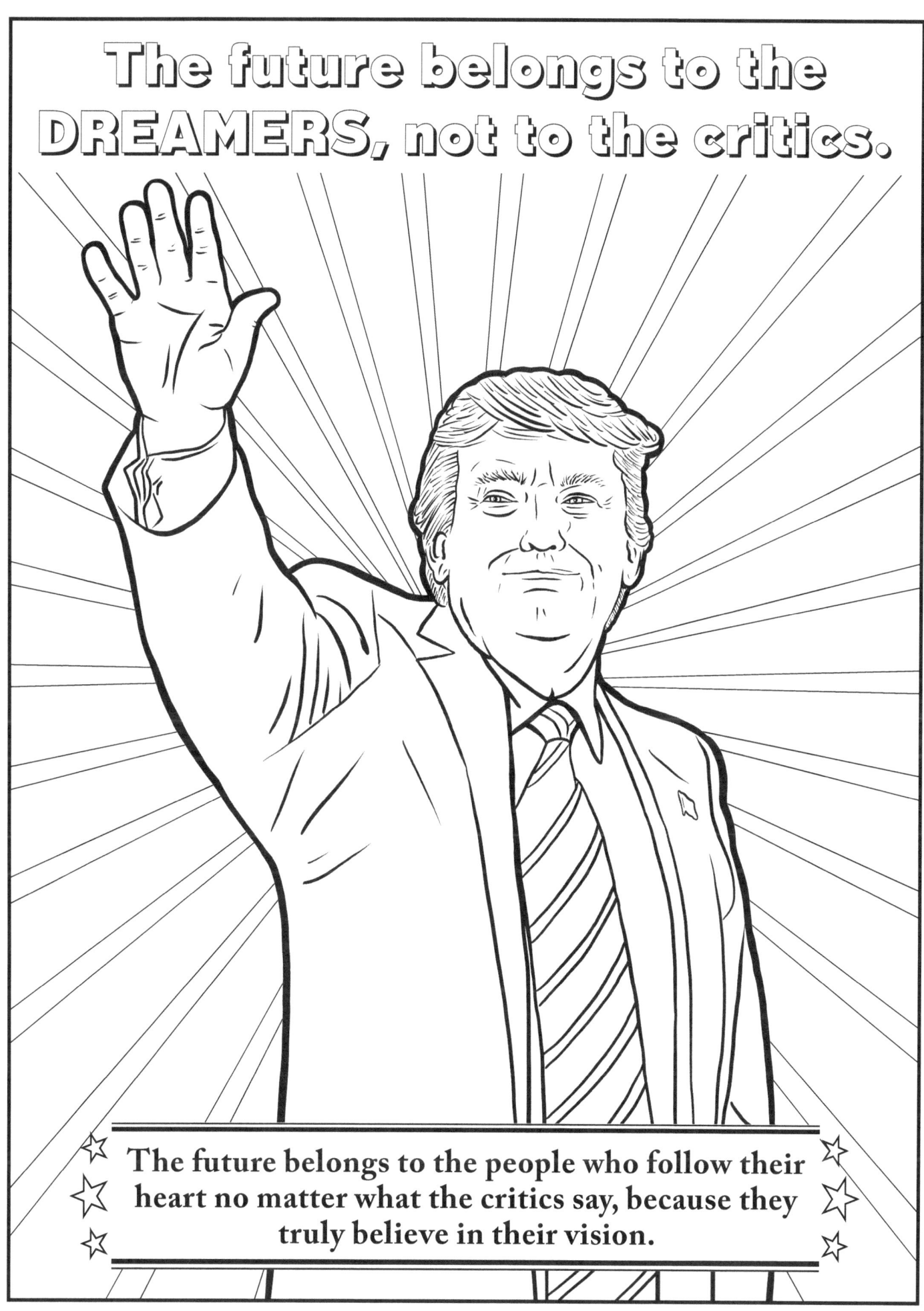

A Note About the Illustrator

I have been working my entire life to try and create something satisfactory, to live free and do things in my own peculiar style. To this end I have created numerous paintings, drawings and other creative work.
In My Great & Unmatched Wisdom is my first self published work, with the help of Amazon and Kindle and the support of the wonderful Monika, my family, friends and the generous people who posted how-to videos online. I view this book simply as a creative project that I enjoyed making and hope others will have fun with. I have no political or ideological alliances, nor am I attempting to make a statement of any kind.

The quotations in this book, allegedly spoken or written or tweeted by President Trump, were gratuitously copied from various sources on the internet (thank you to all who compiled them). I presented them mostly verbatim, with the exception of a word or two.

Again, a huge thank you to President Trump in advance for all 'the best words', which have inspired so many.

Kevin Berggren